The time has come

A STUDY OF JESUS' WORDS AS HE LOOKED AHEAD TO THE CROSS

Beryl Adamsbaum

Contents

Introduction

I have spent most of my life in France, and come from a church tradition that does not normally observe Lent – possibly in reaction to the rather superficial understanding of it that leads to little more than giving up chocolate for six weeks or eating fish rather than meat. It has therefore been a great blessing to me to delve a little more deeply into these very rich chapters of the New Testament in order to prepare this Lent study guide. As we look together at John's Gospel chapters 14 to 17, which implicitly lay out God's plan of salvation, I trust we will come to a deeper understanding of the life and teaching of Christ and the meaning of His sacrifice on the cross, and that we will be drawn closer to Him and also to other believers.

Early in His earthly ministry, Jesus 'appointed twelve – designating them apostles – that they might be with him and that he might send them out to preach and to have authority to drive out demons' (Mark 3:14–15). That little phrase, 'that they might be with him' is so important. Before the apostles were sent out to preach and to heal, they needed to spend time with Jesus, learning from Him, watching how He went about His ministry, observing Him at prayer. Mark records the following incident: 'Very early in the morning, while it was still dark, Jesus got up, left the house and went off to a solitary place, where he prayed' (Mark 1:35). It was at such a time, when 'Jesus was praying in a certain place' (Luke 11:1), that the disciples, who must have been watching Him, had the urge to pray in the same way. This prompted their request that He would teach them to pray too. Jesus taught them what we have come to call 'The Lord's Prayer' (Matt. 6:9–13; Luke 11:2–4).

As we spend time working through this Lent study guide, we too want to 'be with him', in order to assimilate His teaching and enter more deeply and more fully into a relationship with Him. Just like Mary, who 'sat at the Lord's feet' (Luke 10:39), we want to take time out from the busyness of everyday living and sit at Jesus' feet, and quite simply 'be' in the Lord's presence. We want to use these forty days for remembrance, reflection and repentance, as did the Israelites during the forty years they spent in the wilderness. We want to use them for resisting the devil and standing firm on God's Word, as did Jesus during the forty days that He spent in the desert.

Often we think of the Gospels as being straightforward, easy-to-read accounts of the life of Jesus. It is only as we get into them that we realise how difficult some of the issues addressed can be. Jesus' teaching is not always easy to comprehend. A lot of questions that we ourselves might want to ask were already put to Jesus by His disciples, as they expressed to Him their own puzzlement and bewilderment and lack of understanding. As we read through the four Gospels, we see how Jesus teaches His followers and how little by little He reveals to them His true identity: '... the Christ [the Messiah], the Son of the living God' (Matt. 16:16). We notice that His friends are sometimes slow to learn. The four chapters of John's Gospel on which this Lent study guide is based are no exception in that they contain eternal truths that are difficult for our finite minds to grasp. We will see that the disciples often interrupt Jesus to ask for an explanation of His teaching. These chapters help us to see the big picture, as it were. We can become so bogged down with our cares and concerns and responsibilities and occupations that we can easily lose sight of eternal realities. John's Gospel gives us the whole story of how 'The Word became flesh and made his dwelling among us' (John 1:14). Then we learn that Jesus died to save us. He rose again, victorious over sin and death. He has returned to His Father where He is preparing a place for us. He has sent His Holy Spirit to be with and to live in each believer.

One day He will come back and take us to be with Him. 'And so we will be with the Lord for ever' (1 Thess. 4:17).

As you work through these studies, and as you discuss together in your group, pray that your minds will be opened to grasp the meaning of Jesus' words and that, as a result, you will grow in understanding and in your relationship with Him. We are privileged to be able to look upon these episodes with hindsight. We know that after the crucifixion came the resurrection. Jesus' apostles, however, were groping in a fog, as it were. They did not really know what was happening. They had already had the shock (in chapter 13 of John's Gospel) of learning that one of them would betray Jesus, and then of discovering who the betrayer was. Jesus wanted them to understand that events would work together to enable Him to fulfil His mission. He repeatedly spoke to them of His departure, but they were slow to understand.

I have entitled this study guide, *The Time Has Come*. These are the words with which Jesus begins His prayer in John 17:1. 'Father, the time has come …' He says. We might well ask, 'The time has come … for what?' I trust that as you spend time studying and thinking about and discussing and dwelling on these crucial chapters of the New Testament, the answer to that question will become apparent.

The Way, the Truth and the Life

Icebreaker

Consider yourselves to be a group of Jesus' friends, eager to learn from Him (see John 15:14). Introduce yourselves to any members of the group whom you did not previously know. Tell each other a bit about yourselves.

Opening Prayer

Lord, as we begin working through this Lent study guide, please speak to us. We are indeed privileged to be able to read and study these words that You spoke to Your disciples so long ago. Thank You for the precious promises contained in them. Help us to understand Your Word and to appropriate these promises and live in the light of them. We want to draw close to You, Lord, and honour You. We want to spend time in Your presence reflecting and remembering. Show us if there is anything we need to repent of. Help us to resist the devil and stand firm on Your Word.

First Bible Reading
John 14:1–9,12–14

'Do not let your hearts be troubled. Trust in God; trust also in me. In my Father's house are many rooms; if it were not so, I would have told you. I am going there to prepare a place for you. And if I go and prepare a place for you, I will come back and take you to be with me that you also may be where I am. You know the way to the place where I am going.'
Thomas said to him, 'Lord, we don't know where you are going, so how can we know the way?'
Jesus answered, 'I am the way and the truth and the life. No-one comes to the Father except through me. If you really knew me, you would know my Father as well. From now on, you do know him and have seen him.'
Philip said, 'Lord, show us the Father and that will be enough for us.'

Jesus answered: 'Don't you know me, Philip, even after I have been among you such a long time? Anyone who has seen me has seen the Father. How can you say, "Show us the Father"? ... I tell you the truth, anyone who has faith in me will do what I have been doing. He will do even greater things than these, because I am going to the Father. And I will do whatever you ask in my name, so that the Son may bring glory to the Father. You may ask me for anything in my name, and I will do it.'

Setting the Scene

What a privilege to have these words of Jesus! In John's Gospel, chapters 14 to 16, Jesus is talking to His friends. We can overhear a conversation between Jesus and His disciples. We are able to listen in to Jesus' teaching as He prepares His apostles for His death and resurrection and the coming of the Holy Spirit. Some difficult issues are raised and the disciples ask many questions. We notice their expressions of surprise and perplexity as they question Jesus about some of His statements that they find difficult to understand. Jesus explains to His disciples that He will leave them and go to His Father. There He will prepare a place for them and come back so that they may be with Him. Then comes chapter 17, where I feel as if I am walking on holy ground. What a thrill to draw so close that we can hear Jesus praying to His Father!

We sometimes tend to live this life as though it is all there is. And it is true that in our own human experience, this world and this life are all that we have ever known. With our finite minds it is not easy for us to grasp eternal realities. But the Bible clearly teaches that the eternal, invisible God created the world and then came in the Person of His Son to live on this earth as a Man among human beings, in order to pay the price for our sin. 'The Word became flesh and made his dwelling among us' (John 1:14). He then returned to the Father to prepare a place for us. He has promised: 'I will come back and take you to be with me that you also may be where I am' (John 14:3). We need to see our lives in this perspective of eternity. Then I think the words of Jesus will become clearer to us.

Session Focus

The apostle Paul states without ambiguity, 'If only for this life we have hope in Christ, we are to be pitied more than all men' (1 Cor. 15:19). The words of Jesus that we have just read in John 14 lift us up and enable us to see beyond this life. Jesus shows Himself to His disciples – and to us – in His humanity, but He also reveals something of His divine nature. 'Trust in God; trust also in me,' He says (v.1), putting himself on a par with God, and therefore implicitly claiming deity. He endorses this reality in verse 7 as He identifies Himself with the Father: 'If you really knew me, you would know my Father as well. From now on, you do know him and have seen him.' Similarly, what He says to Philip leaves us in no doubt of His true identity: 'Anyone who has seen me has seen the Father' (v.9).

Jesus exhorts His friends to trust so that their hearts will not be troubled. I'm sure we can all identify with troubled thoughts and anxious feelings. 'Cast all your anxiety on him because he cares for you,' writes the apostle Peter (1 Pet. 5:7). And the apostle Paul says, 'Do not be anxious about anything, but in everything, by prayer and petition, with thanksgiving, present your requests to God. And the peace of God, which transcends all understanding, will guard your hearts and your minds in Christ Jesus' (Phil. 4:6–7). Did you notice those two little words 'with thanksgiving'? A thankful attitude towards God as we pray can transform our feelings of anxiety and open up the way for us to receive His peace.

But let us try to put ourselves in the place of those early

disciples. Why might they be worried and upset? Because Jesus was about to leave them. He had told them that He would only be with them a little longer. He added, 'Where I am going, you cannot come' (John 13:33). In answer to Peter's question, 'Lord, where are you going?', Jesus replied, 'Where I am going, you cannot follow now, but you will follow later' (John 13:36). He then explains to them in chapter 14 that He is going to His Father's house to prepare a place for His followers. Then He will come back and take them to be with Him. What a wonderful perspective to look forward to! We can rejoice with the same anticipation. One day we too will live forever with Jesus in His Father's house.

We can be thankful for Thomas' question in verse 5 – which incidentally shows how little he had understood – because Jesus' answer gives expression to one of the great truths of Scripture. 'How can we know the way?' asks Thomas. 'I am the way and the truth and the life,' says Jesus. 'No-one comes to the Father except through me' (v.6). Jesus is the only means of access to the Father. He reveals the Father to us, so that to know Him assures our acceptance by the Father. Jesus gives spiritual life, eternal life, everlasting life, abundant life to all who trust in Him.

Following on from Thomas' question is Philip's request – 'Lord, show us the Father' (v.8) – which shows how slow he, too, is to understand. I don't know about you, but I feel that I'm in good company! Jesus takes the trouble to explain over and over again what the disciples found so hard to grasp. 'Anyone who has seen me,' He says, 'has seen the Father' (v.9). How can we get our finite minds round a spiritual reality such as this? I think that such a revelation should cause us quite simply to worship!

Discussion Starters

1. How did Jesus comfort His disciples in verses 1–4? In what ways do His words encourage you?

   _____

   _____

   _____

   _____

2. Where was Jesus going (v.4)?

   _____

   _____

   _____

   _____

3. Express in your own words Jesus' answer (in verse 6) to Thomas' question in verse 5.

   _____

   _____

   _____

   _____

4. Learn by heart Jesus' response in verse 6. How do these words speak to you personally?

   _____

   _____

   _____

   _____

5. How did Jesus respond to Philip's request in verse 8? What relevance does His response have to you?

_____

_____

_____

_____

6. What did Jesus mean when He said, '... anyone who has faith in me will do what I have been doing. He will do even greater things than these ...' (v.12)?

_____

_____

_____

_____

7. What does it mean to ask in Jesus' name (see verses 13 and 14)? What is the result of asking in Jesus' name? How does this correspond to your experience?

_____

_____

_____

_____

8. What first attracted you to Jesus? Share with the group how you came to put your trust in Him.

_____

_____

_____

_____

Closing Prayer

Thank You, Lord, that You are 'the way and the truth and the life', and that You are preparing a place for us in Your Father's house. Thank You that You are coming back to take us to be with You. Help us to trust You at all times. Thank You for promising us Your peace.

Final Thoughts

'Trust in God; trust also in me,' says Jesus. Surely trust is at the heart of our relationship with the Lord. We may not understand everything we read in the Bible. We may have questions, just as the disciples had questions, but if we have come to a saving faith in Jesus, we will learn to trust Him at all times. We will trust Him for the present and for the future. We will trust Him in the good times and the bad. Jesus indicated to the disciples that if they trusted Him, their hearts would no longer be troubled. They would not be afraid. He would give them His peace. 'Trust in the LORD with all your heart and lean not on your own understanding; in all your ways acknowledge him, and he will make your paths straight' (Prov. 3:5–6). And the psalmist says: '… the LORD's unfailing love surrounds the man who trusts in him' (Psa. 32:10). How wonderful to be able to come to Him in times of anxiety, stress and trouble of any kind and cast our cares on Him, knowing that He who is 'the way and the truth and the life' loves us and will keep us in His peace. 'O LORD Almighty, blessed is the man who trusts in you' (Psa. 84:12).

Trust and obey!
For there's no other way
To be happy in Jesus,
But to trust and obey.

John Henry Sammis (1846–1919)

Further Study

Acts 4:12; Philippians 2:5–11.

Love and Obedience

Icebreaker

In your experience, what prompts people to obey (or disobey) commands, orders, rules, instructions and laws? (For example, children/parents; students/teachers; citizens/laws; motorists/road signs etc.)

Opening Prayer

Thank You, Lord, for Your love for me. Thank You for Your Holy Spirit who will be with me for ever. Give me a deepening consciousness and awareness of Your presence within me. Thank You for the new life that I have in You. Thank You too for the peace that You give me. Help me not to be troubled and afraid, but to trust You at all times. Thank You that You are coming back again. Help me, Lord, to obey You and trust You always. I love You, Lord.

Bible Reading
John 14:15–21,25–27

'If you love me, you will obey what I command. And I will ask the Father, and he will give you another Counsellor to be with you for ever – the Spirit of truth. The world cannot accept him, because it neither sees him nor knows him. But you know him, for he lives with you and will be in you. I will not leave you as orphans; I will come to you. Before long, the world will not see me any more, but you will see me. Because I live, you also will live. On that day you will realise that I am in my Father, and you are in me, and I am in you. Whoever has my commands and obeys them, he is the one who loves me. He who loves me will be loved by my Father, and I too will love him and show myself to him ... All this I have spoken while still with you. But the Counsellor, the Holy Spirit, whom the Father will send in my name, will teach you all things and remind you of everything I have said to you. Peace I leave with you; my peace I give you. I do not give to you as the world gives. Do not let your hearts be troubled and do not be afraid.'

Setting the Scene

We concluded last week's study with the chorus, 'Trust and obey'. Last week we concentrated more on the aspect of trust. This week we are going to look more closely at the theme of obedience.

Do I love God? Do you love God? That might be a difficult question to answer. How do we know if we really love God? One test we can apply is whether or not we want to please Him. I think desiring to please Him would be a sign of our love for Him. And how best can we please Him? By obeying Him.

When John talks about love, he does not look upon it as a feeling or an emotion, but as something intensely practical. What is true love according to the Bible? Paul's words to the Corinthians best describe it:

Love is patient, love is kind. It does not envy, it does not boast, it is not proud. It is not rude, it is not self-seeking, it is not easily angered, it keeps no record of wrongs. Love does not delight in evil but rejoices with the truth. It always protects, always trusts, always hopes, always perseveres. Love never fails.

(1 Cor. 13:4–8).

Obedience is the test of our love for God. John makes a strong connection between love and obedience, both here in his Gospel and also in his letters. Our passage this week begins with Jesus' words, 'If you love me, you will obey what I command' (v.15). Then again in verse 21 we read, 'Whoever has my commands and obeys them, he is the one who loves me.' In the next chapter – chapter 15 – Jesus says, 'If you obey my commands, you will remain in my love ...' (v.10). In his first letter, John writes, 'This is love for God: to obey his commands' (1 John 5:3). And in his second letter, we read, 'And this is love: that we walk in obedience to his commands' (2 John 6).

Throughout the Bible there is an emphasis on love – God's love for us, our love for God and our love for other believers. All these different aspects are closely linked. And, of course, Jesus also tells us to love our enemies (Matt. 5:44; Luke 6:27,35).

Session Focus

In this week's passage, Jesus continues speaking to His disciples about His coming departure. Anticipating how they would feel – bereft, alone, abandoned, destitute – Jesus tells them that they need not feel that way. Having told them that He is going away and returning to His Father, in order to reassure them He explains that He will not leave them 'as orphans' (v.18). 'I will come to you,' he says (v.18). What is not really clear is whether Jesus is referring here to His post-resurrection appearances or to some later event. It must have been wonderful for the disciples to see the risen Christ and to know that He was alive for evermore. However, after the resurrection, His appearances were brief and over a short period of time. So is Jesus rather referring to His coming in the Person of the Holy Spirit? Or – a third possibility – is He talking about His return at the end of the age when He will take His followers to be with Him? Maybe each of these phases is implicit in that wonderfully encouraging statement: 'I am coming back to you.'

'… I will ask the Father,' He says, 'and he will give you another Counsellor to be with you for ever …' (v.16). And who is this 'Counsellor'? 'The Spirit of truth', says Jesus (v.17). The word 'Counsellor' comes from the Greek word *parakletos*, which is in fact a difficult word to translate, as it includes so many concepts. As well as 'Counsellor', it can be translated 'Comforter' or 'Advocate' or 'Helper'. These are all names given to the Holy Spirit and they help us to understand something of His role. Jesus tells His followers that this Counsellor – the Spirit of truth or the Holy Spirit (see v.26) – will not only be with them, He will also be 'in' them (v.17). He then explains to His followers more about what the Holy Spirit will do: '... the Holy Spirit ... will teach you all things and will remind you of everything I have said to you' (v.26). During His earthly ministry, Jesus had said many things that His disciples failed to understand. The Holy Spirit would remind them of Jesus' words and give them understanding.

'On that day' (v.20), the day when Jesus will have returned to the Father and sent the Spirit to be with and in the disciples (see verse 17), they will realise fully what He had been talking about, because it would all have become true in their own experience. How important it is that Jesus' teaching does not remain simply abstract truth, but that it becomes real to us in our own experience and that we live it out.

Then Jesus repeats those words with which this chapter began: 'Do not let your hearts be troubled' (v.27). Instead of being troubled and afraid and worried and upset, we can have peace, the peace that Jesus gives. This peace does not depend on our outward circumstances. It is an integral part of our salvation. We have peace with God, because our sins have been forgiven. That overflows into the whole of our being. In our last session we quoted the apostle Paul's words in Philippians 4:6–7. They are so encouraging that they are worth quoting again this week:

> Do not be anxious about anything, but in everything, by prayer and petition, with thanksgiving, present your requests to God. And the peace of God, which transcends all understanding, will guard your hearts and your minds in Christ Jesus.

Just as God later came to live in those early disciples through His Holy Spirit, so He indwells every believer today. I don't know if you have ever stopped to reflect on this mind-boggling truth. If you are a Christian, a child of God through faith in Jesus, then He lives in you in the Person of His Spirit. Take some time now to dwell silently on this overwhelming reality and try to understand the implications of it.

Discussion Starters

1. What connection does Jesus make between love and obedience? See also John 15:9–17.

   _____

   _____

   _____

   _____

2. What will the followers of Jesus realise 'on that day' (v.20)? When do you think 'that day' is?

   _____

   _____

   _____

   _____

3. What teaching about the Trinity can you discern in this passage?

   _____

   _____

   _____

   _____

4. Who will stand in for Jesus while He is away? See also John 15:26.

_____
_____
_____
_____

5. What is the role of the Counsellor?

_____
_____
_____
_____

6. Pick out the verses from this passage which indicate that God lives in the believer in the Person of His Spirit.

_____
_____
_____
_____

7. How do you react to such a truth? To what extent do you tend to be aware of it? How can you become more aware of it? How should this realisation affect the way you live, the way you think, the way you act, the way you speak?

_____
_____
_____
_____

8. Read together aloud John 14:27. What is the difference between the peace that Jesus gives and peace as the world gives? Share with the group specific situations when these words of Jesus might be a comfort to you. Learn this verse by heart, so as to be able to call to mind these words of Jesus in the different experiences of life.

_____

_____

_____

_____

Closing Prayer

Lord, give me a deepening consciousness and a growing awareness of Your Spirit within me. May this wonderful truth not be reduced to words on paper, but may it be a vibrant reality in my life. Lord, I really want Your Spirit to direct me and control me. Thank You for giving me Your peace.

Final Thoughts

Peace, perfect peace, in this dark world of sin?
The blood of Jesus whispers peace within.

Peace, perfect peace, by thronging duties pressed?
To do the will of Jesus, this is rest.

Peace, perfect peace, with sorrows surging round?
In Jesus' presence naught but calm is found.

Peace, perfect peace, with loved ones far away?
In Jesus' keeping we are safe, and they.

Peace, perfect peace, our future all unknown?
Jesus we know, and He is on the throne.

Peace, perfect peace, death shadowing us and ours?
Jesus has vanquished death and all its powers.

It is enough: earth's struggles soon shall cease,
And Jesus call us to heaven's perfect peace.
Edward Henry Bickersteth (1825–1906)

Further Study
1 John 4:7–21.

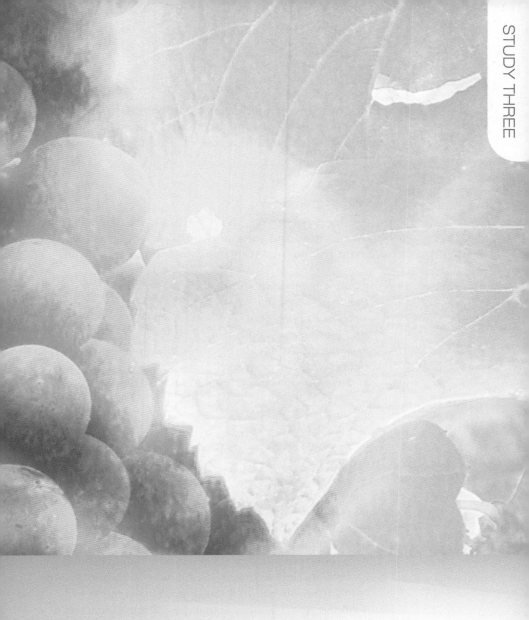

Fruit That Will Last

Icebreaker

From your own experience of gardening, explain the difference between simply cutting off branches and pruning. What is the purpose of pruning, and what are the results?

Opening Prayer

Keep me close to You, Lord. I want to bear much fruit to Your glory, and I know that this is only possible as I remain in You and Your words remain in me.

Cleanse me from my sin, Lord,
Put Thy power within, Lord,
Take me as I am, Lord,
And make me all Thine own;
Keep me day by day, Lord
Underneath Thy sway, Lord,
Make my heart Thy palace and Thy royal throne.

R. Hudson Pope[1]

Bible Reading

John 15:1–8

'I am the true vine, and my Father is the gardener. He cuts off every branch in me that bears no fruit, while every branch that does bear fruit he prunes so that it will be even more fruitful. You are already clean because of the word I have spoken to you. Remain in me, and I will remain in you. No branch can bear fruit by itself; it must remain in the vine. Neither can you bear fruit unless you remain in me.
'I am the vine; you are the branches. If a man remains in me and I in him, he will bear much fruit; apart from me you can do nothing. If anyone does not remain in me, he is like a branch that is thrown away and withers; such branches are picked up, thrown into the fire and burned. If you remain in me and my words remain in you, ask

whatever you wish, and it will be given you. This is to my Father's glory, that you bear much fruit, showing yourselves to be my disciples.'

Setting the Scene

Near where I live in France and just over the border in Switzerland, vineyards stretch in some areas as far as the eye can see. My husband, who is a keen photographer, has immortalised many of these scenes throughout the different seasons. My favourite photographs are ones he has taken in the autumn, with bunches of ripe grapes still on the vine, enhanced by the red and gold leaves.

The picture of the vine is found throughout Scripture and often symbolises God's people. 'Israel was a spreading vine …' says Hosea (Hosea 10:1). In Isaiah's account of 'new heavens and a new earth' (Isa. 65:17), we read that God's people 'will plant vineyards and eat their fruit' (v.21). And Zechariah states that 'The seed will grow well, the vine will yield its fruit, the ground will produce its crops, and the heavens will drop their dew' (Zech. 8:12). Sadly, we also read that, in spite of all the care given to it, it turned into 'a corrupt, wild vine' (Jer. 2:21); 'it yielded only bad fruit' (Isa. 5:2) and became useless (Ezek. 15:1–8). Because His people had been unfaithful, the Lord said, 'As I have given the wood of the vine among the trees of the forest as fuel for the fire, so will I treat the people living in Jerusalem' (v.6).

In stark contrast, Jesus now presents Himself as 'the true vine' (John 15:1), in contrast to the degenerate vine that the Old Testament prophets spoke of. He is the genuine Vine, the real One. This week's passage stresses the importance of fruit-bearing. Our fruitfulness as believers depends, not on our own efforts, but on our remaining in Christ. 'Apart from me you can do nothing,' says Jesus (v.5). The apostle Paul gives us the corollary to that statement: 'I can do everything through him who gives me strength' (Phil. 4:13). As the Father has a key role to play in the fruit-bearing process (John 15:2), it will be to His glory that we bear much fruit.

Session Focus

Like much of Jesus' teaching, these verses in John chapter 15 about the vine initially seem to give a fairly straightforward picture. Jesus is the Vine; His Father is the Gardener; His disciples are the branches. The Gardener cuts off the branches that do not bear fruit. Then they are burned. He prunes the branches that do bear fruit, so that they will yield even more fruit. Jesus states what seems fairly obvious – that no branch can bear fruit by itself; it must remain in the vine. He parallels this observation with the statement that His followers cannot of themselves bear fruit; they must 'remain' in Him. There is a certain form of reciprocity and mutuality between the Christian's remaining in Christ and the Lord's words remaining in the Christian. This is a condition for answered prayer: 'If you remain in me and my words remain in you, ask whatever you wish, and it will be given you' (v.7). The fruit that a Christian bears is proof of his discipleship and brings glory to God.

However, once we start to dig a little deeper, we realise that there are certain aspects that may not be all that easy for us to grasp or that may not correspond exactly to our experience. What about answered prayer, for example? If we do not always experience the answers that we would like or the answers that we expect, maybe we have not yet grasped the full extent of what it means to 'remain' in Christ and to have His words remain in us. And if the disciples are the branches, how come some of them are cut off and burned? That is perhaps because not all those who claim to be followers of Jesus really are His disciples. This picture should bring home to us the need to remain in vital contact with Christ and His Word in order for us to be 'clean' (v.3) and bear fruit.

I wonder what you understand by the verb 'remain'? Other Bible versions enlarge on the meaning by paraphrasing it as follows: 'remain in union with' or 'remain united'. Other translations convey the meaning as: 'abide', 'stay joined', 'dwell', 'live', 'stay' ... So what does it mean to remain in Christ? As I have been thinking about this in the light of the metaphor of the vine and the branches, I would suggest that to remain in Christ means to be firmly attached to Him, to have a vital connection with Him. J.B. Phillips paraphrases it as follows, using the verb 'to grow': 'You must go on growing in me and I will grow in you. For just as the branch cannot bear any fruit unless it shares the life of the vine, so you can produce nothing unless you go on growing in me.' This allegory of the vine underlines the importance of fruitfulness in the Christian life. It brings out the fact that the fruit we bear is not the result of human achievement but of remaining firmly attached to Christ. The fruit we bear is proof of our discipleship. What kind of fruit are we to bear? I would say that as our 'fruit' comes from our attachment to the Vine, it must in some measure be a reflection of the life of Christ in us. Maybe it could be summed up by what the apostle Paul calls 'the fruit of the Spirit': 'love, joy, peace, patience, kindness, goodness, faithfulness, gentleness and self-control' (Gal. 5:22–23). And Paul prays that the Philippians might be 'filled with the fruit of righteousness that comes through Jesus Christ' (Phil. 1:11).

Discussion Starters

1. In the metaphor that Jesus uses, who is the vine, who is the gardener, and who are the branches? What is the role of each of these?

_____
_____
_____
_____

2. What two things are necessary for a branch to bear fruit (vv.1–4)?

_____
_____
_____
_____

3. What happens to branches that do not bear fruit? How might this motivate you to remain firmly attached to the Vine?

_____
_____
_____
_____

4. How can the illustration of the vine and the branches be applied to Jesus and His followers (vv.5–6)? What does it mean to 'remain' in Jesus?

_____
_____
_____
_____

5. Share with the group any experience of 'pruning' in your own life (a painful experience which has had a positive outcome and resulted in spiritual growth).

_____
_____
_____
_____

6. What does Jesus teach about prayer in this passage?

_____
_____
_____
_____

7. What proof of discipleship does Jesus evoke in verse 8?

_____
_____
_____
_____

8. Discuss what kind of fruit you think we are expected to bear.

_____
_____
_____
_____

Final Thoughts

In order to better understand these first eight verses of John chapter 15, we really need to read the next eight verses (vv.9–16) as well. There are numerous parallels between these two passages. In the section we have just studied, Jesus expresses a metaphorical intimacy between Himself and His followers. He is the Vine; His followers are the branches. The next part (vv.9–16) reveals the nature of this intimacy. 'As the Father has loved me, so have I loved you,' says Jesus (15:9). Can we really grasp the depth of that wonderful statement? Believers enjoy something of the intimacy with Jesus that Jesus Himself experiences with His Father.

> *Amazing love! How can it be*
> *That Thou, my God, shouldst die for me?*
> Charles Wesley (1707–1788)

As in last week's study, we note the link between love and obedience. Just as Jesus remains in the Father's love by means of obedience, so the believer must remain in Christ's love by means of obedience. And Jesus adds the further element of joy. 'I have told you this so that my joy may be in you and that your joy may be complete,' He says (v.11). Spend some time meditating on the source and extent of complete joy.

Further Study

Psalm 80:8–16.

Note

1. R. Hudson Pope, 'Cleanse me from my sin, Lord',
   copyright © SGM Lifewords. Used by permission.

Chosen Out of the World

Icebreaker

Discuss with the group the meaning of the expression to 'go astray'? Give some examples of ways in which this expression might be used. To whom or what could it apply?

Opening Prayer

Dear heavenly Father, we would like to bring before You those who are being persecuted for their faith. Please strengthen and sustain them. Give them the courage to live for You in adverse and hostile conditions. Keep their eyes fixed on You. Make them very conscious of Your presence with them. Protect them and their families. Keep them faithful. May Your Word go forth in power. May many more people in the world put their trust in You and come to believe that Jesus died for them. Lord, enable us to keep ourselves from being 'polluted by the world' (James 1:27). Keep us faithful in testifying about You.

Bible Reading

John 15:18–21,25–27

'If the world hates you, keep in mind that it hated me first. If you belonged to the world, it would love you as its own. As it is, you do not belong to the world, but I have chosen you out of the world. That is why the world hates you. Remember the words I spoke to you: "No servant is greater than his master." If they persecuted me, they will persecute you also. If they obeyed my teaching, they will obey yours also. They will treat you this way because of my name, for they do not know the One who sent me. … But this is to fulfil what is written in their Law: "They hated me without reason."

'When the Counsellor comes, whom I will send to you from the Father, the Spirit of truth who goes out from the Father, he will testify about me. And you also must testify, for you have been with me from the beginning.'

John 16:1–4

'All this I have told you so that you will not go astray. They will put you out of the synagogue; in fact, a time is coming when anyone who kills you will think he is offering a service to God. They will do such things because they have not known the Father or me. I have told you this, so that when the time comes you will remember that I warned you. I did not tell you this at first because I was with you.'

Setting the Scene

In the passages that we have looked at already, Jesus has talked a lot about love – the Father's love for Him, His love for His followers, our love for each other. Now He speaks of the opposite: hatred. Before departing from His disciples, Jesus leaves them under no illusion: following Him is going to be costly. They will be hated by 'the world' because of their allegiance to Jesus. This could – and in many cases would – result in persecution. 'The world' used in this sense includes all that is in rebellion against God.

If we belong to Jesus, we do not belong to the world. The world will then become hostile to us. We will face opposition because of our faith. Is this something we are conscious of? Even if our own particular situation is not too uncomfortable at present, we have only to glance a little further afield to become aware of the 'Persecuted Church'. I seem to be getting more and more emails from Christian organisations that work in areas where followers of Jesus Christ are being discriminated against. They are experiencing the cost of following Christ. Many Christians are undergoing torture and even martyrdom.

Let us not become complacent, though, in our comfortable Western society. 'Money', 'sex' and 'power' are three words that are sometimes used to describe the aims and desires of worldly people today. Our newspapers are full of tales of materialism, shady business dealings, selfish ambition, pride and sexual immorality. How do we as Christians stand up against these deviations? By taking note of Jesus' words to His disciples. He reminded them that He had chosen them 'out of the world' (John 15:19). He warned them of the difficulties that would come their way. And His purpose in preparing them was so that they would not 'go astray' (16:1). Let us, too, heed His warning. Let us stand firm against the temptations and persecutions of the world.

Session Focus

As Christians, we identify fully with Jesus Christ. He is our Lord and Saviour, our Master. We belong to Him. We want to live for Him. As the apostle Paul says, 'We are ... Christ's ambassadors ...' (2 Cor. 5:20). Living for Him will invite opposition.

There are many recorded instances in the Gospels of opposition to Jesus. Very early in His ministry, we read that the Jewish religious leaders 'began to plot with the Herodians how they might kill Jesus' (Mark 3:6). Jesus explains why the world hates His followers, just as it first hated Him. It is because He has chosen us out of the world, and for that reason we no longer belong to the world (John 15:20). The world will treat Christians in the same way as it treated Christ. If we do not experience any hostility from the world, then maybe we should examine our discipleship. Am I truly committed to Jesus Christ? Do I really seek to follow Him?

Then Jesus turns the disciples' thoughts from the rather negative aspect of enduring hatred to the positive ministry of testifying about Him. He returns to the subject of 'the Counsellor ... the Spirit of truth' (v.26), first mentioned in chapter 14. Here, in chapter 15, Jesus refers to the Holy Spirit's role as a witness. The disciples will testify along with Him. This is the task of all who profess to follow Jesus.

I was struck recently – when reading the incident of the healing of a demon-possessed man in Mark's Gospel – by the example that this man is to all believers. Once the man had been healed and was 'in his right mind' (Mark 5:15), he begged to go with Jesus. However, 'Jesus did not let him, but said, "Go home to your family and tell them how much the Lord has done for you, and how he has had mercy on you." So the man went away and began to tell in the Decapolis [the Ten Cities] how much Jesus had done for him' (Mark 5:19–20). Surely this is exactly what we are all called to do, to tell people how much the Lord has done for us.

How do you go about this responsibility – or should I rather say, this privilege – of testifying about Jesus? Let us take courage from the fact that the Holy Spirit is directly involved in this work with us. Or rather, we are involved in this work with Him! The testifying and the opposition often go together. Jesus told His disciples, '… when they arrest you, do not worry about what to say or how to say it. At that time you will be given what to say, for it will not be you speaking, but the Spirit of your Father speaking through you' (Matt. 10:19–20). We have instances in the book of Acts where the apostles testified by saying, 'We are witnesses of these things, and so is the Holy Spirit …' (Acts 5:32). Immediately afterwards we read that some of the religious leaders 'were furious and wanted to put them to death' (v.33). In the following chapter, Stephen faced opposition from Jewish leaders, '… but they could not stand up against his wisdom or the Spirit by whom he spoke' (6:10). Soon afterwards he was stoned to death.

In John 16:1–4, Jesus returns to the subject of persecution. Why do you think He warned His disciples of these hard times to come? It was certainly so that they would not be taken unawares. It was so that they would be prepared. And, being ready, they would stand firm. They would not 'go astray' (John 16:1). May we too be prepared for opposition, for hatred and maybe even for persecution.

Let us, as the Spirit inspires us, testify about Jesus as we look forward to that time when He will come back to take us to be with Him.

Discussion Starters

1. How would you define 'the world' in this context (15:18–19)?

   _____
   _____
   _____
   _____

2. In which areas might Christians today be tempted to compromise with worldly schemes or even to be assimilated into 'the world'? How can we make a stand against such temptations?

   _____
   _____
   _____
   _____

3. Why does 'the world' hate those who follow Jesus (15:18–25)? Do you have the impression that 'the world' hates you? In what ways have you personally noticed hostility?

   _____
   _____
   _____
   _____

4. What do you understand by the verb 'testify' (15:26–27)? Share with the group some of the experiences you have had of testifying.

_____
_____
_____
_____

5. What does Jesus warn His disciples of in 16:1–4? Why?

_____
_____
_____
_____

6. How can we best be prepared to face opposition and even persecution?

_____
_____
_____
_____

7. Why might the disciples have been tempted to 'go astray' (16:1). Have you ever been tempted to 'go astray'? If so, for what reason? What kept you from going astray? Or, if you did go astray, what brought you back?

_____
_____
_____
_____

8. How can you see the truth of 16:2 being worked out in practice in world events today?

_____

_____

_____

_____

Closing Prayer
Lord, keep us faithful to You no matter what hostility we might face from those who do not acknowledge You. Keep us from going astray. Give us wisdom and discernment and love and understanding as we seek to share with others what You have done for us.

Final Thoughts
Is there no hope for the world? As I've been preparing this study, one verse has come constantly to my mind. It is probably the first Bible verse that I learned by heart when I was a little girl in Africa. It is there that I first heard – from a missionary family – the good news that Jesus loved me enough to die for me. You have probably guessed by now which verse I am referring to. It is recorded for us in the third chapter of John's Gospel. Jesus is speaking to Nicodemus, and He says, 'For God so loved the world that he gave his one and only Son, that whoever believes in him shall not perish but have eternal life' (v.16). Of course, in those far-off days (in the 1950s), I learned this verse in the King James (or Authorised) Version: 'For God so loved the world, that he gave his only begotten Son, that whosoever believeth in him should not perish, but have everlasting life.' While it is good to learn Bible verses by heart, the words can sometimes become so familiar that the deep meaning escapes us. In thinking about the world that is so hostile to God, I have been marvelling at the fact that God

loved the world – those people in rebellion against Him – enough to die for them. He loved them 'so much that he gave his only Son' (GNB). So, is there hope for the world? Of course there is!

Further Study
James 4:4; 1 John 4:4–6.

Grief and Joy

Icebreaker

'It is for your good' is a phrase that we probably often heard when we were children. Maybe we have used it with our own children. What sort of memories – negative and/or positive – does it conjure up?

Opening Prayer

Lord, we know that we can trust You even if we don't understand all that You say in Your Word. All will happen as You have foretold. We praise You, heavenly Father, that one day we will see You face to face and there will be joy in Your presence. In the meantime, may we be faithful witnesses, as we count on Your Holy Spirit to convict people of sin and to draw them to Yourself. Thank You for the joy of our salvation, even as we face grief and suffering in the world.

Bible Reading
John 16:7–11,16–20

'... I tell you the truth: It is for your good that I am going away. Unless I go away, the Counsellor will not come to you; but if I go, I will send him to you. When he comes, he will convict the world of guilt in regard to sin and right-eousness and judgment: in regard to sin, because men do not believe in me; in regard to righteousness, because I am going to the Father, where you can see me no longer; and in regard to judgment, because the prince of this world now stands condemned ...

'In a little while you will see me no more, and then after a little while you will see me.'

Some of his disciples said to one another, 'What does he mean by saying, "In a little while you will see me no more, and then after a little while you will see me," and "Because I am going to the Father"?' They kept asking, 'What does he mean by "a little while"? We don't understand what he is saying.'

Jesus saw that they wanted to ask him about this, so he said to them, 'Are you asking one another what I meant when I said, "In a little while you will see me no more, and then after a little while you will see me"? I tell you the truth, you will weep and mourn while the world rejoices. You will grieve, but your grief will turn to joy.'

Setting the Scene

Grief and joy may seem completely incompatible to us, but there are many Bible passages where grief and joy are mentioned together. In his first letter, Peter writes: 'In this you greatly rejoice, though now for a little while you may have had to suffer grief in all kinds of trials' (1 Pet. 1:6). When he says, 'In this you greatly rejoice', he refers to something he had mentioned earlier: the 'new birth into a living hope through the resurrection of Jesus Christ from the dead, and into an inheritance that can never perish, spoil or fade' (vv.3–4). That can never be taken away from us; it is ours for the whole of eternity, and it causes us great joy. We must live our lives in the wider perspective of eternity and see beyond our current pain and grief. Peter also says that even our trials can have a positive outcome. They act like a refiner's fire, to test and strengthen our faith (see v.7). James says basically the same thing: 'Consider it pure joy … whenever you face trials of many kinds, because you know that the testing of your faith develops perseverance' (James 1:2–3).

Jesus says, 'In this world you will have trouble. But take heart! I have overcome the world' (John 16:33). As we go through the suffering that this life brings, we can rejoice in our salvation. The concept of salvation includes so much: forgiveness from sin, new life – eternal life – in Christ, the indwelling of the Holy Spirit, the assurance of spending eternity in the Lord's presence, where there will be 'no more death or mourning or crying or pain' (Rev. 21:4). What a lot we can rejoice in!

In John 16:16–20, Jesus continues preparing His disciples for His departure. In mentioning their grief, He implicitly refers to the cross. They will have to face up to the fact of His crucifixion. It is via the cross that Jesus will return to His Father. Only then will the Holy Spirit come to indwell the believers and convict the world.

Session Focus

I wonder how you react to that amazing statement that Jesus made to His disciples, 'It is for your good that I am going away' (John 16:7)? How could it possibly be for their good? Jesus chose His disciples, you remember, so 'that they might be with him' (Mark 3:14). Now He says He is going to leave them! I am sure there was no way that they could see His departure as being beneficial to them. They needed Him. They wanted to have Him close to them. He had taught them many things. They wanted to learn more. And now He tells them that He is going away! How must they have felt? Abandoned? Rejected? Afraid? Insecure? I'm sure you can identify in one way or another with all those feelings.

Well, what did Jesus mean when He said, 'It is for your good that I am going away'? He explains in the very next sentence: 'Unless I go away, the Counsellor will not come to you; but if I go, I will send him to you.' The Counsellor (the Holy Spirit), whom Jesus had already mentioned to His disciples (see chapters 14 and 15), would only come when Jesus went away. He would teach them all things and remind them of things that Jesus had already told them (14:26). Jesus had already explained to His disciples that the Holy Spirit would testify about Him. He added, 'And you also must testify ...' (15:27). Now He explains that it is the Counsellor, living in the disciples, who 'will convict the world of guilt' (16:8).

In last week's study (John 15), we referred to the fact that Jesus' followers are to be witnesses in a world where they will be hated and may also be persecuted. We also mentioned that they are not alone, but that the Holy Spirit is with them and in them. If you are a disciple of Jesus, then His Spirit lives in you and will convict people through your testimony. This is very encouraging, because it means that even if we are not sure how to express ourselves or how best to witness, we can count on the Holy Spirit to do the convicting.

Here (in verses 7–11) Jesus goes into more detail as to the role and ministry of the Counsellor. In fact, the Holy Spirit takes over the work that Jesus Himself had been doing during His earthly ministry. The Holy Spirit has a very positive role, because if He convicts a person, it is surely in order to bring that person through to conversion. Without His intervention, a person would remain enslaved in his sins, imprisoned by the world. It is the Holy Spirit, through the disciples' testimony, who convicts people of sin, of their own self-righteousness and of a judgment that is false.

If people do not believe in Jesus, there is no way their sins can be forgiven, so the Holy Spirit convicts them of their sin of unbelief. What is the righteousness that the Holy Spirit convicts people of? Probably the self-righteousness of 'the world'. The Gospels give us many examples of this kind of righteousness, particularly among the religious leaders. The apostle Paul refers to the fact that, as the Jews 'did not know the righteousness that comes from God and sought to establish their own, they did not submit to God's righteousness' (Rom. 10:3). As Jesus leaves this world to return to the Father, it is the Holy Spirit who takes over the work of convicting the world of its self-righteous attitude. The Counsellor also convicts the world 'in regard to judgment'. What kind of judgment? Probably false judgment due to the world's sinful nature. Again, we see multiple instances of false judgment reported in the Gospels. To take just one example, in John 7:24 Jesus tells the crowd to 'stop judging by mere appearances, and make a right judgment.' The condemnation of Jesus would be the supreme example of this kind of false judgment.

Discussion Starters

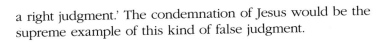

1. How can it be for the disciples' good that Jesus is going away?

   _____
   _____
   _____
   _____

2. What do you do when you feel abandoned, rejected, afraid or insecure?

   _____
   _____
   _____
   _____

3. Try to express in your own words what Jesus said the 'Counsellor' (the Holy Spirit) would do when He came. How much of this corresponds to your own experience?

   _____
   _____
   _____
   _____

4. What exactly does the Holy Spirit convict people of (8–11)?

_____
_____
_____
_____

5. How far can you identify with the disciples' perplexity in verses 17 and 18?

_____
_____
_____
_____

6. What do you think Jesus meant when He said, 'In a little while you will see me no more, and then after a little while you will see me' (vv.16–19)?

_____
_____
_____
_____

7. By means of an illustration, Jesus explains (in verse 21) to the disciples that their grief would turn to joy. Why is this illustration particularly apt? Can you think of other possible illustrations?

_____
_____
_____
_____

8. Share experiences you may have had when your grief turned to joy. How or why did this happen?

_____

_____

_____

_____

Closing Prayer

I would like to suggest that you pray – either silently or by sharing names in your group – for people on your heart who do not yet know Jesus. Pray for opportunities to witness to them. Pray that the Holy Spirit will convict them and that they will come to put their trust in the Lord.

Final Thoughts

The minds of the disciples are full of confusion. Jesus can see that they are upset, but at this point He does not give them much more clarification concerning what He has been sharing with them. Rather, He concentrates on their feelings. Right now they are puzzled. Perhaps they are afraid as well, as Jesus had also mentioned the fact that they would be persecuted (15:20; 16:2). Later they would 'weep and mourn'; they would grieve deeply. Jesus prepares them for their state of grief and assures them that they will emerge from the grieving process. Their 'grief will turn to joy'. The fact is, the pain and loss the disciples experienced when Jesus was crucified gave way to joy as they later met with the risen Christ. They began to see that all that Jesus had been preparing them for was falling into place.

Jesus did not at any time suggest that the disciples should not grieve. Their grief turned to joy as they began to see their circumstances and the historical events of the time in the wider perspective of eternity. May we have that same perspective as we learn to cope with grief and pain and loss in this life. May we draw comfort from the fact that Jesus is with us in the Person of His Spirit and that we will spend eternity with Him.

Further Study

Read John 19:16–30 and Acts 1:8–9; 2:1–4 to see how some of what Jesus had been preparing His disciples for was fulfilled.

Glory!

Icebreaker

Looking at it from different perspectives, discuss ways in which you might understand and explain the meaning of the word 'glory'.

Opening Prayer

Immortal, invisible, God only wise,
In light inaccessible hid from our eyes,
Most blessèd, most glorious, the Ancient of Days,
Almighty, victorious, Thy great name we praise.

Great Father of glory, pure Father of light,
Thine angels adore Thee, all veiling their sight;
All laud we would render, O help us to see
'Tis only the splendour of light hideth Thee.
                Walter Chalmers Smith (1824–1908)

Heavenly Father, thank You for revealing Yourself to us. Teach us to pray, Lord, just as You taught Your early disciples. May we learn from You what sort of things should take priority in our praying. Help us to love one another, and may we truly be united with other believers. Give us a wider vision and a deeper perspective of life and eternity. May we bring You glory as we seek to do Your will.

Bible Reading
John 17:1–6,9,20–21

After Jesus said this, he looked towards heaven and prayed:

'Father, the time has come. Glorify your Son, that your Son may glorify you. For you granted him authority over all people that he might give eternal life to all those you have given him. Now this is eternal life: that they may know you, the only true God, and Jesus Christ, whom you have

sent. I have brought you glory on earth by completing
the work you gave me to do. And now, Father, glorify me
in your presence with the glory I had with you before
the world began.
I have revealed you to those whom you gave me out
of the world …
I pray for them. I am not praying for the world, but for
those you have given me, for they are yours …
My prayer is not for them alone. I pray also for those who
will believe in me through their message, that all of them
may be one, Father, just as you are in me and I am in you.
May they also be in us so that the world may believe that
you have sent me.'

Setting the Scene

We mentioned in the introduction to this series of Lent
studies that Jesus often went to a 'solitary' place in order to
spend time with His Father in prayer. We are not usually
informed as to what exactly passed between Jesus and His
Father. Most of the time Jesus was alone with God and
His prayers were not overheard by anyone. It is not often
that the content of His prayers is revealed to us, except
for brief extracts. For example, in Matthew 11:25–26, Jesus
prays in these words: 'I praise you, Father, Lord of heaven
and earth, because you have hidden these things from the
wise and learned, and revealed them to little children. Yes,
Father, for this was your good pleasure.' Similarly, in John
11:41, after raising Lazarus from the dead, Jesus prays in
public: 'Father, I thank you that you have heard me. I knew
that you always hear me, but I said this for the benefit of
the people standing here, that they may believe that you
sent me.' Just before the cross, Jesus twice asks His Father
if 'the cup' might be taken from Him, and concludes His
prayer with 'may your will be done' (Matt. 26:39,42).

Here in John chapter 17, however, we hear Jesus talk to
His Father at some length. Following on immediately from

His words to His disciples in chapters 14 to 16, Jesus, still in the presence of His followers, 'looked towards heaven and prayed' (17:1). The disciples were immensely privileged to overhear the words He spoke to His Father. And we are also privileged to have the content of Jesus' prayer recorded for us.

There are three distinct parts to Jesus' prayer. In the first five verses Jesus prays that He may be glorified and that He may glorify God; in verses 6–19 He prays for His disciples; and in verses 20–26 He prays for all believers.

Session Focus

There are several themes running through Jesus' prayer. There is the theme of unity, for example, as Jesus prays that all those who believe in Him may be one. He compares this with the oneness that He and His Father have. This unity is something that all Christians throughout the world today – 'from every tribe and language and people and nation' (Rev. 5:9) – should be experiencing. Then the theme of the world comes up again, as Jesus implies that this lived-out unity among believers will be instrumental in the world's coming to faith in Christ. This is quite a challenge! Are we living out the answer to Jesus' prayer? In other words, are we living in unity with other believers to the extent that the world might see Jesus in us and be drawn to Him?

One of the words that Jesus repeats several times in His prayer is the word 'glory'. What do you think of when you hear the word 'glory'? Does it convey to you something of splendour, majesty, radiance and shining light? It could mean all or any of those things. In the New Testament, the Greek word *doxa* (translated 'glory') means the outshining of the inner being and is chiefly used to describe the revelation of the character and presence of God as seen in the Person and work of Jesus Christ.

In the Old Testament, Moses said to God, '... show me your glory' (Exod. 33:18), and God replied, '... you cannot see my face, for no-one may see me and live' (v.20). In 1 Timothy 6:16, the apostle Paul mentions the fact that God 'lives in unapproachable light, whom no-one has seen or can see'. Yet God revealed Himself in His Son Jesus Christ: 'No one has ever seen God. The only Son, who is the same as God and is at the Father's side, he has made him known' (John 1:18, GNB). A few verses earlier John made it clear that 'The Word [Jesus] became flesh and made his dwelling among us. We have seen his glory ...' (v.14). Leon Morris, in his commentary on the Gospel of John, writes that here 'John is speaking of that glory that was seen in the literal, physical Jesus of Nazareth. As He came in lowliness we have an example of the paradox that John uses so forcefully later in the Gospel, that the true glory is seen, not in outward splendour, but in the lowliness with which the Son of God lived for men and suffered for them ... It is the cross of shame that manifests the true glory.'[1]

When He entered Jerusalem for the Passover, Jesus predicted His own death. He said, 'The hour has come for the Son of Man to be glorified' (John 12:23). And He prayed, 'Father, glorify your name!' (John 12:28). Here, in John 17, He echoes that same prayer: 'Glorify your Son, that your Son may glorify you ... I have brought you glory on earth by completing the work you gave me to do. And now, Father, glorify me in your presence with the glory I had with you before the world began' (vv.1,4–5). In His earthly mission, Jesus laid His glory aside, only to take it up again when His work was done. It was at the cross that Christ completed the work He came to do, and so brought glory to God. We read (in John 19:28,30) that 'knowing that all was now completed, and so that the Scripture would be fulfilled ... Jesus said, "It is finished."' He finished the work He came to do. He accomplished the ministry for which He was destined. He fulfilled the purpose for which He became man. In so doing, He glorified God.

> *Turn your eyes upon Jesus,*
> *Look full in His wonderful face;*
> *And the things of earth*
> *Will grow strangely dim*
> *In the light of his glory and grace.*
>
> Helen H. Lemmell[2]

Discussion Starters

1. How would you define eternal life? (See verse 3.)

_____

_____

_____

_____

2. How did Jesus glorify God (v.4)?

_____

_____

_____

_____

3. How can we glorify God?

_____

_____

_____

_____

4. How would Jesus be glorified (vv.1,5)?

_____

_____

_____

_____

5. In verses 20–26 Jesus prays for all believers. What is the essence of His prayer?

_____

_____

_____

_____

6. In your experience, are Christians united? What can we do to encourage greater unity among believers?

_____

_____

_____

_____

7. How did Jesus complete the work that He came to do?

_____

_____

_____

_____

8. How does it make you feel to know that Jesus prays for you?

_____

_____

_____

_____

Closing Prayer

Speak, Lord, in the stillness,
While I wait on Thee;
Hushed my heart to listen
In expectancy.

Speak, O blessed Master,
In this quiet hour;
Let me see Thy face, Lord,
Feel Thy touch of power.

For the words Thou speakest,
'They are life' indeed;
Living Bread from heaven,
Now my spirit feed!

All to Thee is yielded,
I am not my own;
Blissful, glad surrender –
I am Thine alone.

Speak, Thy servant heareth!
Be not silent, Lord;
Waits my soul upon Thee
For the quickening word!

Fill me with the knowledge
Of Thy glorious will;
All Thine own good pleasure
In Thy child fulfil.

E. May Grimes (1868–1927)

Final Thoughts

And so we come back to those words with which Jesus began His prayer: 'Father, the time has come' (John 17:1). Having worked through these studies, we are hopefully now better able to answer the question that we posed in the introduction: 'The time has come ... for what?' Perhaps the best way to understand it would be to see first of all examples in John's Gospel where Jesus says in fact the opposite: 'My time has not yet come' (John 2:4; 7:6,8,30; 8:20). In these examples, He was still near the beginning of His earthly ministry. It was not yet time for Him to leave this world and return to the Father. He had not yet completed what He came to do. It was not yet time for Him to be glorified.

However, as we read through John's Gospel, we see that, as from chapter 12, Jesus is conscious that His 'time has come'. In John 12:23 we read, 'The hour has come for the Son of Man to be glorified.' In John 13:1, we read: 'Jesus knew that the time had come for him to leave this world and go to the Father.' In John 17:4, He says that He has completed His work. He has fulfilled God's purposes. And He did it for you. He did it for me.

O make me understand it,
Help me to take it in,
What it meant to Thee, the Holy One,
To bear away my sin.

Katherine Agnes May Kelly (1869–1942)

Further Study

Don't leave it there! Read John chapters 20 and 21 and meet with the risen Christ.

Notes

1. Leon Morris, *The Gospel According to John* (Grand Rapids, Michigan: Eerdmans, 1975) p.104.
2. Helen H. Lemmell, 'Turn your eyes upon Jesus'. All reasonable effort made to find the copyright holder of this hymn.

Leader's Notes

If you have never led a study before, you may feel quite
nervous. Then you are in good company! Moses realised
his inadequacy when God called him to lead His people
out of Egypt. Joshua must have been trembling in his
shoes when he took over from Moses. God told him to
be 'strong and courageous' and He gave him a wonderful
promise: '... I myself will be with you' (Deut. 31:23).
Jeremiah said to God, '... I do not know how to speak; I
am only a child' (Jer. 1:6). Even the apostle Paul admitted
to the Corinthians: 'I came to you in weakness and fear,
and with much trembling' (1 Cor. 2:3). Whether you feel
intimidated or not, count on God's presence with you and
on His enabling and equipping as you lead the group.

Each study needs careful and prayerful preparation by
the leader of the group. Pray for understanding of the
passage. Pray for wisdom and sensitivity in leading the
group. Pray for the members of the group. Pray that God
will speak to you all through His Word. Be prepared to
rephrase the questions in order to encourage participation.
Leave enough time for all to contribute. Encourage
discussion by asking questions such as, 'What do the rest
of you think?' or 'Has anyone anything to add?' Don't be
afraid of silence. Give people the time to think. Try to
get a balance between encouraging shy or timid people
to participate and discouraging too talkative members
from monopolising the discussion. The icebreaker at the
beginning of each study is aimed at encouraging the
members of the group to feel comfortable with each other
and to interact with each other before launching into a
study of the Bible passage. Do not spend more than a few
minutes on the icebreaker.

You could ask different members of the group to read the
different sections of each study. For example, someone
could read the opening prayer; another person, the

Bible passage; yet another person the section entitled 'Setting the Scene', and so on, right through to the 'Final Thoughts'. There might be times when it could be appropriate to read aloud together one of the prayers or a quote from a song/hymn.

Study One: The Way, the Truth and the Life

Aim of the Session

To understand Jesus' words to His disciples and to appropriate the promises He made to them. Jesus told His disciples that He was going back to His Father. He told them not to be worried and upset. He would prepare a place for His followers in His Father's house. He would come back and take them (and us) to be with Him. Try to see 'the big picture'. We want to assimilate Jesus' teaching and live in the light of His promises. We want to learn to trust Him.

Discussion Starters

2. Jesus was going back to His Father – via the cross, the resurrection and the ascension. Make sure all these different events are brought out in your group discussion.

3. Try to put yourselves in Thomas' place. How far can you identify with his puzzlement and lack of understanding?

6. After Jesus had returned to His Father, His disciples, full of the Holy Spirit, were instrumental in the conversion of many (eg Acts 2:41). They also did miracles of healing (eg Acts 14:8–10). Paul brought Eutychus back to life (Acts 20:9–10). The works that the disciples did after Jesus' resurrection and ascension were not greater in kind than those He had done Himself during His time on earth. However, Jesus was limited by space and time. He lived in a fairly restricted geographical area and died a young man. The disciples covered a wider area geographically and had a greater sphere of influence.

7. To do something or to ask something 'in the name of' someone is not a simple formula. It means that what we do or what we ask for will be in accordance with all that the person who bears the name stands for. If we ask for something in Jesus' name, our request must be consistent with Jesus' character and be in accordance with what He would want. Note that the result will be to bring glory to God.

Study Two: Love and Obedience

Aim of the Session
To get to grips with the fact that, as Christians, we are indwelt by the Spirit of God. What difference should this make in our lives? How should it affect our thoughts, words, attitudes, deeds, plans, purposes, relationships ...?

Discussion Starters
2. 'On that day' probably refers to the day when the resurrected Christ would have returned to His Father and sent the Holy Spirit to be with the disciples. The second part of the verse ('... you are in me, and I am in you') would lead us to suppose that Jesus extends the thought to the time when He would be permanently present with all believers. 'The resurrection of Jesus and His presence with His own points unmistakably to the continuity of the divine life which flows from the Father, through the Son, and in the Church.'[1]

3. The word 'Trinity' does not appear in the Bible. In this passage (John 14:15–21,25–27), teaching about what we call the Trinity (the three Persons of the Godhead – Father, Son and Holy Spirit) is implicit insofar as Jesus (the Son) says that He will ask the Father to send His Spirit. The fact that Jesus talks of 'another' Counsellor (v.16) must mean that there is already one, and that can only be Himself. It is by the Spirit that the Father and Son are present with and in believers.

Study Three: Fruit That Will Last

Aim of the Session
To learn how we can bear fruit to God's glory.

Discussion Starters
I would strongly recommend that, together with this week's passage (John 15:1–8), you read as a group the following paragraph (John 15:9–16). These verses complement the teaching in verses 1–8. 'John 15:9–16 deals with the nature of the intimacy between Jesus and the believer, between the vine and the branch … and … is simultaneously the exposition of the main themes of 15:1–8, and an answer to the perplexities of the latter.'[2]

Study Four: Chosen Out of the World

Aim of the Session
To prepare us to face opposition as we try to live for Jesus and as we testify about Him. Following Him can be costly. This session could also make us more conscious of believers who are being persecuted for their faith and lead us to pray for them.

Icebreaker
It might be worth spending a little longer on this particular icebreaker. Try to bring out the importance of following Jesus' teaching, in order not to go astray. Jesus says that the aim of His teaching was to prevent the disciples from going astray (16:1). We find the expression again in Proverbs chapter 5 (v.23) and chapter 7 (v.21), in relation to adultery. 'Keep my commands'; 'guard my teachings' (Prov. 7:2)

would be the antidote to going astray. The prophet Jeremiah noted that God's people '... have been lost sheep; their shepherds have led them astray ...' (Jer. 50:6). However, God Himself says, '... the people of Israel will no longer stray from me ...' (Ezek. 14:11).

Discussion Starters

1. 'The world' in this context refers to all those who do not profess to follow Jesus, and who are hostile to Him and opposed to Him and therefore to His followers as well.

4. To testify or to bear witness means to tell what Jesus has done for us, so that others may also come to believe and put their trust in Him. This passage links very closely the witness of the disciples with the convicting work of the Holy Spirit.

Study Five: Grief and Joy

Aim of the Session

To get to grips with the role and ministry of the Holy Spirit as He is at work through the believer, and to try to recognise that the conflicting and contradictory emotions of grief and joy each have a legitimate place in our lives. We can still 'greatly rejoice' (1 Pet. 1:6) in our salvation even in times of pain and sadness.

Discussion Starters

6. The disciples are not the only ones who are bewildered by what Jesus says here. His words have puzzled many people since. Jesus uses the phrase 'a little while' twice in verse 16. The disciples pick up on this expression in verses 17 and 18 and wonder what Jesus meant by it. The first time He uses it ('In a little while you will see me no more ...'), He is surely referring to His approaching death on the cross. The second time He uses it ('... after a little while you will see me'), I would think He is probably referring to His post-resurrection appearances. However, as the disciples quote Jesus as having said, 'Because I am going to the Father' (v.17), it is possible that the second mention of the 'little while' refers to the coming of the Holy Spirit. There is also the possibility that Jesus is already referring to His second coming.

Study Six: Glory!

Aim of the Session
To see how Jesus was glorified and how He brought glory to His Father.

Discussion Starters
1. It may be helpful to look up some other verses referring to eternal life. Some suggestions are as follows: Luke 18:18–30; John 3:16; 5:24; 6:40,47; Rom. 6:22; 1 Tim. 1:15–16. The adjective 'eternal' does not only mean that life goes on for ever. It also refers to the quality of life. Eternal life is God's life lived out in the believer.

2. Bring out the fact that true glory is via the way of the cross. (This is relevant as well for questions 3 and 4.)

3. Glory as the world understands it is often equated with fame, prestige, celebrity, money, status, position and possessions. Jesus had none of these. He didn't even have anywhere 'to lay his head' (Matt. 8:20). If we are to be faithful followers of Christ, we will live in contradiction to what the world thinks, teaches and aspires to. Jesus said, 'If anyone would come after me, he must deny himself and take up his cross daily and follow me' (Luke 9:23). That's where our glory lies – in dying to ourselves and giving Jesus first place in our lives. For us, true glory lies in the path of lowly service, wherever that might lead. It could lead to persecution. It could lead to death. But death is not the end. With the eyes of faith, we can look beyond the sufferings of this life to that 'eternal glory' (2 Cor. 4:17) that will be ours in heaven.

5. If you have time, read the whole of Jesus' prayer for all believers (vv.20–26).

6. The unity of which Jesus speaks is a reflection of the unity – the perfect unity – that exists between the Father and the Son. Unity among true believers already exists and is real, even if it is not perfect. We are all saved by grace; we are all indwelt by the Holy Spirit. But we need to keep close to the Lord and obey His command to love one another.

Notes
1. C.K. Barrett, *The Gospel According to St John* (London: SPCK, 1956) p.388.
2. D.A. Carson, *Jesus and His Friends* (Carlisle: Paternoster Press, 1995) pp.90–91.

National Distributors

UK: (and countries not listed below)
CWR, Waverley Abbey House, Waverley Lane, Farnham, Surrey GU9 8EP.
Tel: (01252) 784700 Outside UK (44) 1252 784700

AUSTRALIA: CMC Australasia, PO Box 519, Belmont, Victoria 3216.
Tel: (03) 5241 3288 Fax: (03) 5241 3290

CANADA: David C Cook Distribution Canada, PO Box 98, 55 Woodslee Avenue, Paris, Ontario N3L 3E5.
Tel: 1800 263 2664

GHANA: Challenge Enterprises of Ghana, PO Box 5723, Accra.
Tel: (021) 222437/223249 Fax: (021) 226227

HONG KONG: Cross Communications Ltd, 1/F, 562A Nathan Road, Kowloon.
Tel: 2780 1188 Fax: 2770 6229

INDIA: Crystal Communications, 10-3-18/4/1, East Marredpalli, Secunderabad – 500026, Andhra Pradesh. Tel/Fax: (040) 27737145

KENYA: Keswick Books and Gifts Ltd, PO Box 10242, Nairobi.
Tel: (02) 331692/226047 Fax: (02) 728557

MALAYSIA: Salvation Book Centre (M) Sdn Bhd, 23 Jalan SS 2/64, 47300 Petaling Jaya, Selangor.
Tel: (03) 78766411/78766797 Fax: (03) 78757066/78756360

NEW ZEALAND: CMC Australasia, PO Box 303298, North Harbour, Auckland 0751.
Tel: 0800 449 408 Fax: 0800 449 049

NIGERIA: FBFM, Helen Baugh House, 96 St Finbarr's College Road, Akoka, Lagos.
Tel: (01) 7747429/4700218/825775/827264

PHILIPPINES: OMF Literature Inc, 776 Boni Avenue, Mandaluyong City.
Tel: (02) 531 2183 Fax: (02) 531 1960

SINGAPORE: Alby Commercial Enterprises Pte Ltd, 95 Kallang Avenue #04-00, AIS Industrial Building, 339420. Tel: (65) 629 27238 Fax: (65) 629 27235

SOUTH AFRICA: Struik Christian Books, 80 MacKenzie Street, PO Box 1144, Cape Town 8000.
Tel: (021) 462 4360 Fax: (021) 461 3612

SRI LANKA: Christombu Publications (Pvt) Ltd, Bartleet House, 65 Braybrooke Place, Colombo 2.
Tel: (9411) 2421073/2447665

TANZANIA: CLC Christian Book Centre, PO Box 1384, Mkwepu Street, Dar es Salaam.
Tel/Fax: (022) 2119439

USA: David C Cook Distribution Canada, PO Box 98, 55 Woodslee Avenue, Paris, Ontario N3L 3E5, Canada. Tel: 1800 263 2664

ZIMBABWE: Word of Life Books (Pvt) Ltd, Christian Media Centre, 8 Aberdeen Road, Avondale, PO Box A480 Avondale, Harare. Tel: (04) 333355 or 091301188

For email addresses, visit the CWR website: www.cwr.org.uk
CWR is a Registered Charity - Number 294387
CWR is a Limited Company registered in England - Registration Number 1990308

Day and Residential Courses
Counselling Training
Leadership Development
Biblical Study Courses
Regional Seminars
Ministry to Women
Daily Devotionals
Books and Videos
Conference Centre

Trusted all Over the World

CWR HAS GAINED A WORLDWIDE reputation as a centre of excellence for Bible-based training and resources. From our headquarters at Waverley Abbey House, Farnham, England, we have been serving God's people for over 40 years with a vision to help apply God's Word to everyday life and relationships. The daily devotional *Every Day with Jesus* is read by nearly a million readers an issue in more than 150 countries, and our unique courses in biblical studies and pastoral care are respected all over the world. Waverley Abbey House provides a conference centre in a tranquil setting.

For free brochures on our seminars and courses, conference facilities, or a catalogue of CWR resources, please contact us at the following address.
CWR, Waverley Abbey House, Waverley Lane, Farnham, Surrey GU9 8EP, UK

Telephone: **+44 (0)1252 784700**
Email: **mail@cwr.org.uk**
Website: **www.cwr.org.uk**

 Applying God's Word
to everyday life and relationships

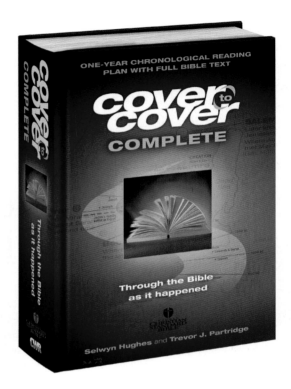

Journey through the whole Bible in one year

These daily Bible readings are set out in the order that events happened, with devotional applications, illustrations and more.

CBC's 2008 reference book of the year!
Cover to Cover Complete
ISBN: 978-1-85345-433-2

Only £19.99 (plus p&p)

Enjoy in-depth Bible study

Each issue of these bimonthly daily Bible reading notes gives you insightful commentary on a book of the Old and New Testaments.

Enjoy contributions from two well-known authors every two months, and over a five-year period you will be taken through the entire Bible.

Only £2.49 each or £12.50 per year subscription, (inc p&p in the UK) from January 2009

Prices correct at time of print

Go deeper into God's Word

These unique resources for group and individual study provide seven stimulating 1–2 hour sessions with icebreakers, Bible readings, discussion starters, personal application and leader's notes.

Revelation 1–3
John Houghton
ISBN: 978-1-85345-461-5

23rd Psalm
Selwyn Hughes with Ian Sewter
ISBN: 978-1-85345-449-3

Philemon
Christopher Brearley
ISBN: 978-1-85345-453-0

The Lord's Prayer
Selwyn Hughes with Ian Sewter
ISBN: 978-1-85345-460-8

The Second Coming: Living in the light of Jesus' return
Selwyn Hughes with Ian Sewter
ISBN: 978-1-85345-422-6

Philippians: Living for the sake of the gospel
John Houghton
ISBN: 978-1-85345-421-9

Genesis 1–11: Foundations of reality
Jeremy Thomson
ISBN: 978-1-85345-404-2

The Letter to the Colossians: In Christ alone
John Houghton
ISBN: 978-1-85345-405-9

Revelation 4–22: The Lamb wins! Christ's final victory
Brian Hoare
ISBN: 978-1-85345-411-0

Prices correct at time of printing

The Prodigal Son: Amazing grace
Rob Frost
ISBN: 978-1-85345-412-7

Fruit of the Spirit: Growing more like Jesus
Selwyn Hughes with Ian Sewter
ISBN: 978-1-85345-375-5

Jeremiah: The passionate prophet
John Houghton
ISBN: 978-1-85345-372-4

The Sermon on the Mount: Life within the new covenant
Chris Leonard
ISBN: 978-1-85345-370-0

Proverbs: Living a life of wisdom
Ruth Valerio
ISBN: 978-1-85345-373-1

Ecclesiastes: Hard questions and spiritual answers
Christopher Brearley
ISBN: 978-1-85345-371-7

1 Corinthians: Growing a Spirit-filled church
Christine Platt
ISBN: 978-1-85345-374-8

Moses: Face to face with God
Elizabeth Rundle
ISBN: 978-1-85345-336-6

2 Timothy and Titus: Vital Christianity
Christine Platt
ISBN: 978-1-85345-338-0

Rivers of Justice: Responding to God's call to righteousness today
Ruth Valerio
ISBN: 978-1-85345-339-7

Nehemiah: Principles for life
Selwyn Hughes with Ian Sewter
ISBN: 978-1-85345-335-9

Only £3.99 each